No Limits

MOUNTAIN BIKING

Jed Morgan

W

FRANKLIN WATTS

LONDON • SYDNEY

First published in 2005 by
Franklin Watts
96 Leonard Street
London
EC2A 4XD

Franklin Watts Australia
45–51 Huntley Street
Alexandria, NSW 2015

© Franklin Watts 2005

Series editor: Adrian Cole
Series design: Pewter Design Associates
Art director: Jonathan Hair
Picture researcher: Sophie Hartley

A CIP catalogue record for this book is available from the British Library.

ISBN: 0 7496 5822 3

Printed in Malaysia

The author and publisher would like to thank the following people for their
contribution to the production of this book: Steve and Jill Behr at Stockfile
(www.stockfile.co.uk), Joe Breeze (www.breezerbikes.com), Pete Webber (www.imba.com),
Gareth and Sam Jefferies (www.endlessride.com), Nicola Wilcockson (www.raleigh.co.uk),
John Chennells (www.orangebikes.co.uk).

Acknowledgements:
© Michael S. Yamashita/ Corbis: 5b. Photo by Wende Cragg: 4t & b, 29b. Courtesy
Endlessride: 5tr, 8t, 10l, 15b, 17t, 21c & b, 26t, 31. Courtesy Endlessride, photo by Sian
Hughes: 18bl. Courtesy Endlessride, photo by Andy McCandlish: 18br. Courtesy
International Mountain Biking Association: 18t. Courtesy Orange Mountain Bikes Limited:
6-7, 8bl, 9t. Courtesy Raleigh Bikes UK: 8br. Sacramento Bee/Jay Mather: 19b.
© Stockfile/Steven Behr: Cover, 7t, 9bl & br, 10r, 11, 12l, c & r, 13, 14t & b, 15t, 16t & b,
17b, 20t & b, 21t, 22t & b, 23t, c & b, 24l & r, 25t, 26b, 27b, 28t, 29t. © Stockfile/Malcolm
Fearon: 5tl, 27t, 28b. © Stockfile/Tom Phillips: 19t. © Stockfile/Chris Ratcliff: 25b.

Impotant Note:

Contents

Mountain bike world

In the past 30 years mountain biking has developed into a multi-billion pound sport. But millions of people also use mountain bikes (MTBs) to get to school, for weekend trips, or just for fun.

The clunker clan

The first MTBs were invented by a group of friends in Marin County, California, USA, in 1976. They adapted a bike by adding gears, a front brake and new wheels with fat tyres, which was called the 'clunker' or 'ballooner'. They became known as the 'clunker clan', and used their home-made bikes to race down nearby Mount Tamalpais.

Joe Breeze

Joe Breeze, a clunker clan member, went on to build the first ever MTB. He introduced the 'Breezer' in 1977. Only ten bikes were made, but his ideas started a new trend. The first factory-produced MTBs such as the 'Stumpjumper' and 'Rockhopper' became available in the early 1980s.

Joe Breeze poses in 1977 with Breezer No.1 – the first purpose-built MTB.

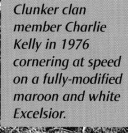

Clunker clan member Charlie Kelly in 1976 cornering at speed on a fully-modified maroon and white Excelsior.

FROM THE EDGE

The first ever MTB Olympic gold medals were won in 1996 by Paola Pezzo (left) of Italy for the women and Bart Brentjens of the Netherlands for the men. Paola Pezzo also won gold in Sydney 2000: 'The Olympics were the best... but winning gold was definitely the highest point. The number one thing to remember [about racing] is to have fun... and enjoy the mountain bike experience.'

A world craze

Mountain bike fever swept around the world as more and more people got involved in this exciting new sport. By the late 1980s mountain bike sales had overtaken those of other bicycles. Mountain bike clubs were started all over the world and races became major attractions for both riders and spectators. In 1990 a World Championship was started, and in 1996 mountain biking became an Olympic sport.

To the limit

* Over 50 million mountain bikes are made and sold every year
* Factories in China, such as the one below, produce the most bikes
* People in the USA buy the most mountain bikes

Know your bike

MTBs may look similar but each part is carefully selected to give the perfect ride. The Orange 223 IBS DH shown here — a World Cup-winning design — has features in common with most MTBs.

To the limit

Over 300 parts go into making an Orange mountain bike. It takes a skilled mechanic around one hour to hand assemble a complete bike.

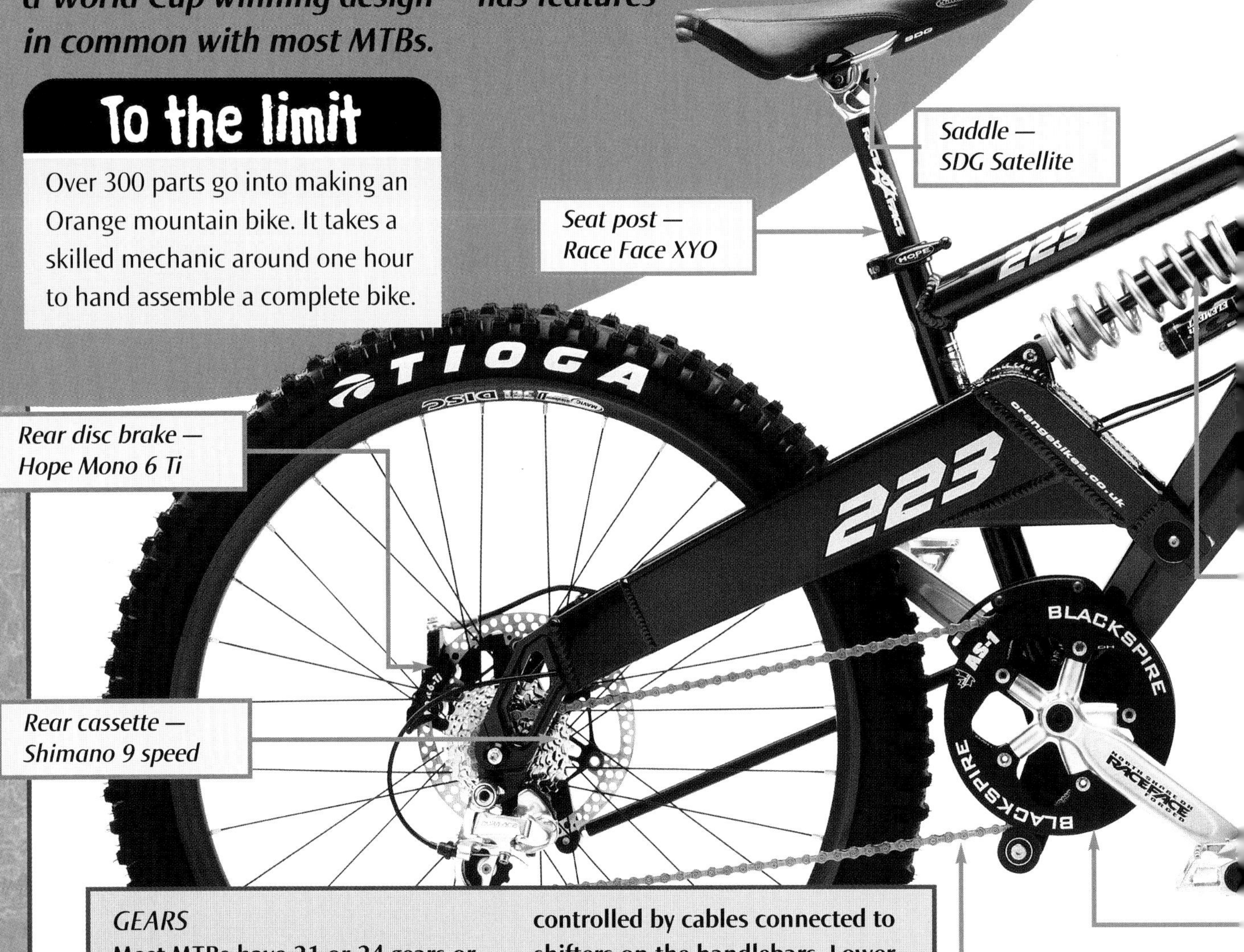
Saddle — SDG Satellite
Seat post — Race Face XYO
Rear disc brake — Hope Mono 6 Ti
Rear cassette — Shimano 9 speed
Chainset
TIOGA
223
orangebikes.co.uk
BLACKSPIRE
AS-1

GEARS

Most MTBs have 21 or 24 gears or 'speeds', with 3 gears at the front (connected to the pedals by a chain ring) and 7 or 8 gears at the back (connected to the hub of the back wheel by the rear cassette). The 223 IBS DH has just 9 gears. The front and back gear sets are connected by the chainset and controlled by cables connected to shifters on the handlebars. Lower gears make it easier to pedal and move. They are good for steep or very bumpy ground. Higher gears need more effort to make the bike move. They are used for high speeds, for example when travelling downhill, or over smooth surfaces.

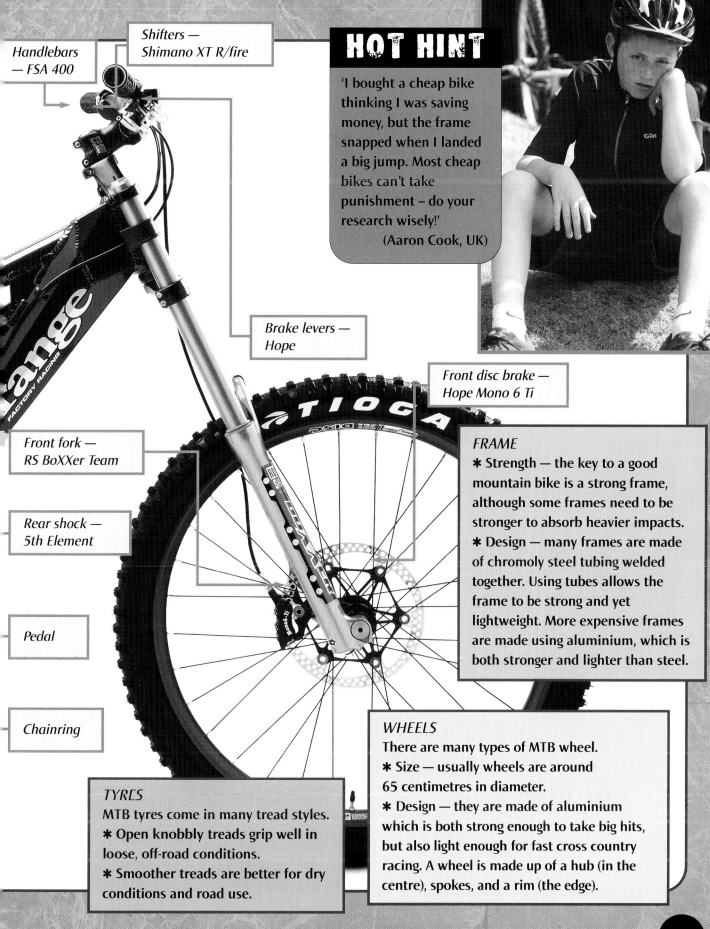

Handlebars
— FSA 400

Shifters —
Shimano XT R/fire

HOT HINT

'I bought a cheap bike thinking I was saving money, but the frame snapped when I landed a big jump. Most cheap bikes can't take punishment – do your research wisely!'
(Aaron Cook, UK)

Brake levers —
Hope

Front disc brake —
Hope Mono 6 Ti

Front fork —
RS BoXXer Team

Rear shock —
5th Element

Pedal

Chainring

FRAME
✱ Strength — the key to a good mountain bike is a strong frame, although some frames need to be stronger to absorb heavier impacts.
✱ Design — many frames are made of chromoly steel tubing welded together. Using tubes allows the frame to be strong and yet lightweight. More expensive frames are made using aluminium, which is both stronger and lighter than steel.

WHEELS
There are many types of MTB wheel.
✱ Size — usually wheels are around 65 centimetres in diameter.
✱ Design — they are made of aluminium which is both strong enough to take big hits, but also light enough for fast cross country racing. A wheel is made up of a hub (in the centre), spokes, and a rim (the edge).

TYRES
MTB tyres come in many tread styles.
✱ Open knobbly treads grip well in loose, off-road conditions.
✱ Smoother treads are better for dry conditions and road use.

A bike for all

Whatever you are looking for in an MTB there is a bike out there for you. Not all mountain bikes are suitable for all uses though, so making the right choice is important.
Always ask at your local bike shop for advice.

Cross country

Cross country (XC)

These bikes are lightweight and can have up to 27 gears. They are very good all-round bikes for off-road cycling and can handle most types of terrain. Most XC bikes have a front suspension and are called 'hardtails'.

Downhill

Downhill MTBs are tough, strong bikes. They have both front and rear shocks to help ride out bumps at high speeds. Downhill bikes also have fewer gears (normally 9). The lack of gears and their weight make them unsuitable for climbing.

Touring

A touring MTB is a mid-weight, all-purpose bike. It is perfect for road or gentle off-road use. They normally have 21 or 24 gears and many now have a front suspension fork. Their frames are designed to take bolt-on luggage racks for carrying equipment.

Downhill

Touring

Cool science

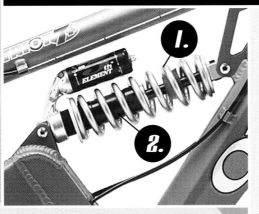

Suspension helps to absorb the impact of a mountain bike going over rough ground. This is done by shock-absorbers or 'shocks', which are made up of a spring (1) and a damper (2). The spring is compressed when the bike takes a hit, but it is the damper – usually filled with a liquid or gas – that controls the speed with which the spring compresses and then rebounds.

Stunt

A stunt MTB has to be super strong to stand up to extra tough treatment. As well as a solid frame they have to be light and easy to manoeuvre. They have fewer gears and may have only one. This is to reduce the chance of parts being damaged by stunt riding. Many models do not even have a saddle because the rider spends most of the time standing on the pedals (see Daniel Comas Riera's bike on page 25).

Freeriding

Freeriding is more a style of riding than a type of bike. Many freeriders choose strong bikes with front and rear shocks – a basic downhill bike – but with a modified suspension and gears. XC bikes can also be used for freeriding. As long as you're having fun and pushing yourself, it doesn't matter what you ride, it's how you ride it.

Stunt

Freeriding

Get geared up

To perform at your best you must have the right MTB gear. It comes in different styles to suit the way you ride, but there are some basics, such as a helmet and gloves, that all riders must have.

Clothing

You can begin enjoying your mountain bike in almost any clothing that you feel comfortable in. Professional mountain bikers normally wear tight-fitting clothing made of artificial fabrics such as Lycra. These provide warmth and comfort, but also allow your body to sweat when it gets hot. Lightweight jackets provide protection in cold or wet weather.

Gloves

A good pair of gloves helps to prevent blisters and protect your hands when you crash. They also help keep your hands warm when riding in the cold. For racing, make sure you buy padded gloves to provide extra protection.

HOT HINT

Make sure you do not wear clothing that is too loose as this could get caught in the chain of your bike and cause a crash. Make sure you tie your shoelaces tightly, too.

Shoes

Lightweight, waterproof shoes are the best type for mountain biking. They should have stiff soles that provide good grip for wet or slippery ground. Some MTB shoes have a cleat system called SPD (see page 24). This allows them to attach to special pedals that are fitted to a bike. These shoes help your body and bike to work as one and give you loads of extra power!

Wearing a helmet is essential, whether you're riding to the shops or, like this rider, on a trail.

The SPD system allows a rider to really bond with his or her bike.

'I was on the tail of my cycling buddy in Washington State jammin' down a twisty single track. We were cruising pretty quick and that's all I remember. When I woke up my buddy was asking if I was OK. I had gone over a ledge and head first into a tree. Thank goodness for helmets – I split the ol' bucket right down the middle!!! Needless to say I have the helmet pieces as a reminder of my luck that day in wearing one......'
Jenny Scott, USA

Downhill riders, like the one shown here grabbing big air, all wear full face helmets, goggles and body armour.

Helmet

A good helmet – or 'brain bucket' – is essential. It provides vital protection when you fall from your bike and could even save your life. There are almost as many styles of helmet as there are different shapes of head, so go to your local bike shop to get a helmet fitted properly. For downhill racing you will need a full face helmet to provide extra protection.

Body armour

Body armour is a good idea for serious freeriding, tricks or racing. Elbow, knee and shin guards offer good protection against most falls. Full body armour is essential for downhill racing because it will protect your ribs and spine in a high-speed wipeout.

To the limit

The phrase 'brain bucket' was used by American soldiers during the Second World War to refer to their steel helmets. MTB helmets today are usually made from polystyrene foam with a polycarbonate shell.

Get ready to ride

There is nothing worse – or more embarrassing – than having your bike break down. Sometimes this cannot be helped, but basic bike care can help to make sure that you keep riding the trail, instead of walking it.

1. Keep it clean

2. Check it out

3. Lube it up

1.

2.

3.

4.

5.

6.

7.

Keep it clean

A dirty bike might look cool, but dirt or 'crud' can damage your bike. You should take time to clean your bike with a mild detergent and water as soon after a ride as possible. Keeping the moving parts, such as wheels, brakes and gears clean is especially important. Little bits of grit can damage your brake pads and wheel rims or brake discs, clog up your gears and even cause your chain to jump.

Check it out

The best way to avoid problems is to check your bike regularly. Check the tyres, brakes and cables for wear and tear and replace them if they are damaged. Make sure the wheel nuts are tight and that the seat and seat post are secure and straight. If you notice that the handlebars or pedals are loose or wonky then get a mechanic at your bike shop to check them over.

The breakdown kit. It is a good idea to carry a multi-tool (3) whenever you ride. On longer trips take a basic breakdown kit in a waterproof bag (4). This should include tyre levers (1), a puncture repair kit (2), a chain tool (5), a spare inner tube (6) (for serious punctures) and a bike pump (7).

HOT HINT

Pre-ride checklist:

1. Make sure the bike is clean and the brakes, gears and chain are free from crud
2. Check the tyres, brakes and cables for signs of wear and replace parts if required. Check the handlebars, pedals and wheels are working correctly and secured properly
3. Lube up the chainset and gears to keep them running smoothly

Lube it up

To keep your bike running smoothly it is important to keep your chainset and gears well lubricated or 'lubed up' with a genuine bike oil (available from bike shops). This helps the parts to move easily and so reduces the effort needed to make the bike move. Check your bike is lubricated before you set off.

Play it safe

Mountain biking is a dangerous sport – thousands of people are injured every year. Even the most careful rider will get minor injuries, but by playing it safe most serious problems can be avoided.

Safety First

The best way to stay safe is to think safe. Check out your bike before you set off on a ride and remember to wear the right gear. Be aware of what is going on around you simply by checking the path ahead and listening for hidden dangers.

Using a map will help you plan a successful trip.

Sharing the experience of a ride can be a great way to make new friends.

Plan your trip

You should always plan where you are going, even if it is just a local trip. For longer trips you must plan your route carefully, especially if you don't know the area. Take a mobile phone with you and let someone know where you are going and when you will be back. If you don't return on time they can use the information to help find you.

Buddies

Mountain biking is best done with at least one buddy. This means you can look out for each other and help if one of you becomes injured. Riding with buddies is also great fun!

Street wise

If you cycle on roads or cycle paths make sure you are clearly seen by others. Lights and bright clothing can help. You should obey traffic rules and signs, and make sure you always give way to pedestrians. Remember: bad riding gives all cyclists a bad name.

Many crossings on cycle routes are shared with pedestrians – so don't forget to give way.

Be prepared

Changes in the weather, breakdowns and hunger can turn a great day into a nightmare. Make sure you are prepared, with the right type of clothing, a tool kit, and snacks and a drink to refuel yourself.

Know your limits

There is no point in trying tricks or tough rides that you do not feel confident about. It is important that you know your limits. Start with the basics and build up to more advanced techniques and rides.

It's important to be realistic about your own abilities. Even experienced riders get off and walk sometimes.

HOT HINT

The staff at your local bike shop don't just sell bikes, they're also a great source of knowledge. So, next time you're there and you have a question, don't be embarrassed to ask for advice.

Just for Fun

Mountain biking is an expensive professional sport, but most people who own a mountain bike ride it just for fun. It's a great way to get together with buddies and explore the local area.

Hiring a bike is a sneaky way to try before you buy!

Try before you buy

In many places it is possible to hire a mountain bike; this way you can try it out before buying one yourself. This can be a good introduction to mountain biking. Many hire centres are located on trails especially designed for mountain bikes so the staff there can even help you plan a route.

Join the club

There are thousands of mountain bike clubs around the world. Some countries have national clubs or associations. One of the longest-running clubs in the UK is the North Wales Mountain Bike Association. They organise races and events throughout the year.

HOT HINT

A mountain bike club provides a perfect opportunity to learn new skills as well as discover new trails and make some good friends. If you can't find a local mountain bike club why not start a new one with your friends?

Many clubs have their own jump spots where riders can hang out.

FROM THE EDGE

'Without doubt the most exhilarating and adrenalin-soaked holiday I've ever been on. .....I've no doubt we will be back.' Holiday guest, endlessride alpine mountain biking holidays (www.endlessride.com). Set up in 2000, endlessride operates holidays for riders like those shown on the right, in one of the most popular European mountain biking destinations: Morzine in the French Alps.

Take a break

Another way to enjoy your mountain bike is to go on a biking holiday. There are many companies that now offer MTB holidays around the world. You can take your own bike or hire one when you are there. It is a great way to explore somewhere new and enjoy your bike at the same time.

Tricks and skills

Once you've mastered riding your mountain bike it can be fun to learn a few tricks. These not only help to improve your skills, but can also look really good. Some of the tricks and stunts that you could try out are shown on pages 22–25.

Developing a good flatland technique, like the one shown here, requires great patience. But this type of trick really boosts your skill level.

The great outdoors

Mountain bikes and the wilderness were made for one another. MTBs are often the best way to explore wild forests, bleak mountains, barren deserts or open plains. They are quiet, and if ridden carefully, cause very little environmental damage.

Hit the trails

Many wilderness areas have trails especially for mountain bikes, others have trails that are shared with hikers and horses. These are carefully planned to take in the best sights and are normally well marked. The trails are often graded by how challenging they are. This means you can start with basic trails and build up to longer or harder ones as you become more experienced.

FROM THE EDGE

INTERNATIONAL MOUNTAIN BICYCLING ASSOCIATION

The IMBA was established in 1988 to encourage low-environmental impact riding and trailwork. Today, its network includes 450 bike clubs. Its guidelines include:

* Ride on open trails only
* Leave no trace; take your rubbish home
* Control your bike at all times
* Always give way to other trail users
* Never spook wildlife or other animals

HOT HINT

Always look ahead for obstacles on the trail – who knows what will be around the next corner.

Riding single-file can help to reduce trail erosion.

FROM THE EDGE

'Suddenly we pulled over the top and a scene of salt flats, volcanoes and blue skies lay before us. Our dream had become a reality! ...It was now time to head back to our familiar world. The 2,000 metre descent down the volcano to our camp was our only real stretch of downhill, so we made the most of it. What had taken us three days to cycle up took us three hours to descend!' Phil Whiting (left) and Tom Phillips, High Andes Mountain Bike Expedition

Expedition rides

Some riders like to experience the great outdoors for several days at a time. Such rides are normally called expedition rides and need very careful planning. On expeditions riders normally carry their sleeping gear and even their food with them. This makes the bikes heavy so riders have to be very fit. A good way to try out an expedition is to join one organised by a club.

Extreme wilderness

Very experienced riders have taken their mountain bikes to some of the most extreme places on Earth. One of the earliest extreme adventures was completed by cousins Nick and Richard Crane from the UK. In 1984 they cycled their mountain bikes to the top of Mt Kilimanjaro – the highest mountain in Africa at 5,895 metres!

To the limit

On 30 November 2001 Orawan (left) and Chareon (right) Othong from Thailand set out on the ultimate outdoor adventure – to mountain bike around the world. They hope to complete their adventure in 2006.

Basic skills

Riding an MTB can be very different from anything you have ever experienced before. The best riders are always in tune with their bike, working together as one.

Balancing

Developing good balance is essential. Get used to balancing by riding in a straight line, or standing still on your pedals. Once you've done that, try some gentle corners. Mastering balance early on will help all your other skills.

This experienced rider is demonstrating some extreme balancing skills.

Learn to lean into corners and position your legs correctly, as shown here.

HOT HINT

A good way to learn cornering techniques is to watch a XC or downhill race. Look at how the riders move their body and bike to take the corners.

Cornering

The key to developing a good cornering technique is to lean your bike into the bend. Bending your inside leg and straightening your outside leg will help you to do this. Do not lean too far though, or your bike may lose its grip and land you in the dirt. You should plan ahead for a corner, too. If you need to slow down then brake before the corner, not while going around it. Speed up again as you exit the corner by pumping hard. Falling off on corners is easier than you think, so practise carefully and you'll be amazed at how quickly you travel.

Braking

Mountain bikes have brakes on the front and rear wheels. To slow down, both brakes should be used with equal force. Too much rear brake and the rear wheel may skid. Too much front brake could lock the front wheel and send you flying Superman-style over the handlebars! Learn to brake smoothly – it is safer and means your brakes and tyres will last longer, too.

Keep alert when riding downhill – obstacles come at you faster at high speed.

Effective braking will help you stay in control of your bike.

Riding downhill

Nothing beats the feeling of hammering downhill, but you must be in control and alert. You will need to stand for most slopes. Straighten your arms and push your weight to the back of the bike, but remember to relax and look ahead. Control your speed using your brakes and keep the pedals level to avoid roots and rocks.

Climbing

Mountain bikes love hills. Their wide tyres give extra grip and their gears mean that even the steepest slope is possible – providing you're fit enough. Look for a good line on the trail and select your gear before you hit the rise. Shift down in good time, pace yourself and sit in the saddle – this keeps the weight over the rear wheel.

FROM THE EDGE

'Beginner or expert, little matches the pride at achieving the peak of a rise, after either a patient slog or a maximum strain. The descent is that much sweeter for it.' Nicky Crowther, The Ultimate Mountain Bike Book

Basic tricks

Tricks are not only useful for showing off. They can also help you on a trail. The best way to learn is from someone who can show you, but all tricks need practice, which will build up your confidence.

Pulling a wheelie

I. A wheelie is one of the first tricks most riders learn. To pull a wheelie you need to pull up on the handlebars and lean your weight back at the same time. This is best done at a slow speed.

HOT HINT

Use a wheelie to negotiate tough drops when you haven't got enough speed to safely clear the end of an obstacle (page 25). Otherwise you may snag your chainring and plant yourself in the dirt.

2. The perfect wheelie takes time to master, so don't worry if you can't do it first time. If your front wheel is coming too high then gently squeeze the rear brake to bring it down slightly. If the wheelie is too low then pull on the handlebars and pedal a little harder to raise the front wheel up into the air.

Grabbing some air

1. Flying over a jump feels great, and it can be done safely by checking the landing area first. To grab air without landing in a heap you must keep control of your bike. As you approach the lip of the jump stand up on your pedals and pull on the handlebars to lift the front of your bike.

HOT HINT

As you improve you can increase the size or the speed of your jump. Look for jumps with steeper lips. And remember that the faster you travel the longer the jump.

2. As the bike leaves the ground try to keep your weight in the centre and relax your arms and legs.

3. Try to land with both wheels at the same time and allow your arms and legs to bend as you land. This will help to absorb the impact of landing. Start with small jumps until you feel confident enough to take on anything tougher.

Advanced tricks

Some advanced tricks are just for show, but others can help you ride higher-grade trails. You should only try more advanced tricks once you have become an expert at the basics.

HOT HINT

Use a bunny hop to avoid obstacles, or add one at the end of your push for big air. Bunny hops and other tricks are easier if you use Shimano Pedalling Dynamics (SPD) pedals and shoes. These clip your feet and pedals together so it is easier to lift the bike into the air.

Bunny hops

1. To do a bunny hop stand on the pedals and crouch low over your bike with your arms and legs bent. When you want to jump, spring your body upwards and pull on the handlebars. As the front wheel lifts up, pull up with your legs and feet to make the back wheel lift off the ground too.

2. When in the air keep your arms and legs relaxed for the landing. You should try and land with both wheels at the same time.

Drop-offs

For a successful drop-off you need to keep your weight balanced. How far you lean back to maintain this depends on the drop. Make sure the drop is not too steep before you go over the edge. You should:

* Look ahead to choose a safe route and take it slowly
* Level up your pedals to stop them snagging
* Lean back so that your bottom is over the rear wheel, without buffing yourself on the tyre!
* Stay relaxed and squeeze your brakes gently
* If in doubt, get off and walk – try it another day
* ADVANCED

You can try doing a drop-off using a wheelie, called a wheelie drop. Once in the air keep your weight central to the bike and try to land on both wheels at the same time.

To the limit

In November 2001 Daniel Comas Riera from Spain made the highest ever bunny hop on a mountain bike. He jumped over a bar 1.16 metres high!

HOT HINT

During a drop-off the further you lean back, the less weight is placed over the front wheels and the less control you have. You have to adjust your centre of gravity by leaning your body. Otherwise, when you move the handlebars, you may find you can't turn properly.

Get serious!

If you get hooked by the mountain bike bug then there are lots of options to get really serious. From local club meetings to international racing, there are no limits to how involved you could become.

Start local

Local mountain bike clubs can be found in most towns all over the world and they always welcome new riders. Joining a club is a great way to get experience. Who knows, if you're good enough you may even get spotted by a talent scout and get offered a sponsorship deal.

The World Cup events, such as the one held at Fort William, Scotland, are great places to see pro riders in action.

A global sport

Mountain biking events now take place around the world throughout the year. The biggest competition is the UCI (Union Cycliste Internationale) World Cup series. It began in 1991 with XC mountain biking, then downhill was added in 1993 and 4X in 2002. Most of the races are held in Europe and North America, but they have also been held in New Zealand, Australia, Japan, Mexico and South Africa. The new 2005 UCI 'Pro Tour' includes the World Cup series.

Racing for the lead at the Olympics. For many XC riders the ultimate goal is to become Olympic champion.

Go for glory!

The ultimate mountain bike events are the annual UCI World Championship and the Olympic Games, which are held every four years. It is these events that all the riders train for and hope to win. The World Championship is held in a different country each year and it is the highlight of the mountain biking calendar.

To the limit

At the Olympics in Athens 2004, the XC event was held at Parnitha Hill. The women's event was won by Norway's Gunn-Rita Dahle. Julien Absalon of France won gold in the men's XC.

Make it to the top

Only the very best will make it to the top, but here are a few tips to help you on your way:

* Start riding as often as you can
* Keep yourself physically fit with general exercise and a healthy diet
* Join a club and learn from those with more experience
* Get involved in races as soon as you can
* Be patient and determined
* Get help and support from your family and friends

Grabbing a snack. Talk to more experienced riders to help improve your skills.

Meet the pros

Mountain biking is a fairly new sport, so many of its earliest pioneers are still around today. For example, Joe Breeze and Gary Fisher, who built and raced the earliest MTBs, are still actively involved in improving bike design.

Turning professional

Pro MTB riders can earn big money and get to travel the world from race to race. However, their lives are not always easy. They must train hard to become super-fit athletes so they can compete at their best. Even then, they often have a relatively short period (maybe 5–6 years) at the top, simply because mountain biking is such a competitive and physical sport. Injuries are common and most riders retire from professional events when they are still in their early 30s.

Crashing out of an event can ruin a season. Pro riders need to remain especially focused.

To the limit
RIDER PROFILE:

Paola Pezzo is an Italian XC rider who is one of the most successful riders ever. She is the only person to have won the MTB 'triple crown' – the World Championship, the World Cup and the Olympics. Pezzo took a break from racing to have a baby, but she was entered for the 2004 Olympics in Athens, although on this occasion she failed to finish.

To the limit

RIDER PROFILE:

Ned Overend from the USA was one of the first riders to make a living from mountain biking, and won many races and two World Championships in the late 1980s. He became known as 'the lung' because of his ability to cycle up the steepest of hills. Today, Ned works for the Specialised mountain bike team, passing on his years of experience to the next generation of mountain bike superstars. He still races MTBs in the Xterra Triathlon Championships (biking combined with swimming and running).

The Pearl Pass clunker tour of 1978. This is just one of many images that appear on the Hall of Fame website (mtnbikehalloffame.com).

Hall of Fame

In 1988 a Mountain Bike Hall of Fame was opened in Boulder, Colorado, USA. It celebrates the history of mountain biking and the key people involved in the sport. There are close to 100 names already in the hall of fame and new faces are added every year. If you succeed in making it to the top, you too could become a member of this exclusive club one day!

Jargon buster

big air — describes a seriously big jump where you spend several seconds in mid air!

bunny hop — a jump that lets you hop – bunny-style – over obstacles, such as fallen branches or potholes, or just for the fun of it.

cassette — holds together the rear gear rings and fixes them to the rear wheel hub.

centre of gravity — an invisible point at which you find your body weight is evenly distributed.

chainset — the part between your pedals and bike frame that holds the chain in place, including the gearing system.

crud — mud, dust, grit, oil, in fact any form of dirt that gets on you or your bike.

Flatland techniques — tricks that are performed on flat ground. They help to develop bike control.

IMBA — the International Mountain Bicycling Association set up in 1988.

jump spot — a cool location where the land makes for good jumping or drop-offs.

Lycra — the tradename for an elastic polyurethane fabric that is used to make mountain bike clothing and other sportswear.

Morzine — a location in the French Alps that is well known as a mountain bike centre.

multi-tool — an all-in-one tool that includes allen keys, screwdrivers and spanners.

polycarbonate — a very strong form of plastic. It is used to make the outer layer of cycle helmets because it is difficult to break. It is also used to make unbreakable windows.

polystyrene — a type of hard foam used in cycle helmets to help cushion your head against any hard impacts.

shifters — a lever or button on the handlebars that allows you to change gear.

snagging — getting caught on obstacles such as branches and rocks.

SPD (Shimano Pedalling Dynamics) — a system that binds your foot to the pedal to give you more power and control. You need special SPD shoes and pedals for this to work.

Speeds — this is the number of gears a bike has. Most bikes are 21 or 24 speed.

sponsorship — when a rider is given money by a MTB team or manufacturer to race in return for promoting their products.

wheelie — riding with the front wheel of the bike in the air.

Find out more

Every effort has been made by the Publishers to ensure that these websites contain no inappropriate or offensive material. However, because of the nature of the Internet, it is impossible to guarantee that the contents of these sites will not be altered. We strongly advise that Internet access is supervised by a responsible adult.

www.nwmba.demon.co.uk

The North Wales Mountain Bike Association is one of the UK's oldest and best known mountain bike clubs. Find out about routes and events all over the UK.

www.imba.com

The International Mountain Bicycling Association website. Find out about the work of the IMBA.

www.raleigh.co.uk

The home of the UK's largest bike manufacturer. Includes guides to looking after your bike as well as the latest bike products.

www.endlessride.com/

Visit this site to find out more about what you could do on a mountain biking holiday.

www.mtnbikehalloffame.com/

The website for the Mountain Bike Hall of Fame. Visit here for some history of mountain biking and a look at some of its biggest stars.

www.exploratorium.edu/cycling/

Learn all about the science behind cycling. It will help you learn about mountain bike materials, gears, brakes and much more besides!

www.orangebikes.co.uk

Find team news, components and clothing to tickle your tastebuds on this site from Orange Mountain Bikes Limited.

www.mountainbike.com/

Mountain Bike on-line magazine. Offers news, gear reviews, interviews and loads of other interesting stuff as well as some great pictures.

www.dirtworld.com

An online information guide for mountain biking. Check out 'trail guide' page for links to some of the best trails in the world. It also has a 'dirty stories' section for tales of mad global adventures to inspire you.

Index